Wish-granting Words

Wish-granting Words

Poems by

Smith Agarwal

RAVI DAYAL Publisher
Delhi

Published by

RAVI DAYAL Publisher
51 E Sujan Singh Park
New Delhi 110003

Distributed by

ORIENT LONGMAN LTD
Bangalore Bhubaneshwar Calcutta Chennai
Ernakulam Guwahati Hyderabad Jaipur
Lucknow Mumbai New Delhi Patna

ISBN 81 7530 046 9

Typeset by Astricks, New Delhi 110070, www.astricks.com
Printed at Pauls Press, New Delhi 110020

Dedicated to my Father
Col. Prabhakar Raj Bahuguna
16 July 1929 – 20 September 1996

Acknowledgements

Acknowledgements are due to the editors of the following periodicals and anthologies in which some of these poems, at times in different versions, first appeared:
Kavya Bharati, The Scoria, Literature Alive, The Journal of the Poetry Society (India), Indian Literature, Indian Review of Books, Wasafiri (London), *Poetry Review* (London), *Ariel* (Canada), *Thumbscrew* (Oxford), *Verse* (U.S.A.), *Poetry India: Voices for the Future*; *Poetry India: Voices in Time; Poetry India: Voices from Within; Poetry India: Voices of Silence*, ed. H.K. Kaul; *Nine Indian Women Poets*, ed. Eunice de Souza, 1997.

I would like to thank the following organizations and people for their continuing encouragement and support: The Poetry Society (India) and the judges of its competitions; The British Council and The Charles Wallace (India) Trust; Ruskin Bond (for publishing my first poems in *Imprint*, Oct. 1976); Adil Jussawala, Keki N. Daruwalla, Eunice de Souza, Arvind Mehrotra, Suniti Namjoshi, K. Satchidanandan, Alok Rai, H.K. Kaul, Richard Walker, Blake Morrison, Ian Duhig, Michael Hulse, Peter Forbes, Anuradha Roy, Rajni, Malashri, Angela, Lyn, Tarun and Geetan Tejpal, Mala and Ravi Dayal, for his skilled editing.

जो रुके तो कोह–ए–गराँ थे हम, जो चले तो जाँ से गुज़र गये
रह–ए–यार हमने क़दम क़दम तुझे यादगार बना दिया

— फ़ैज़ अहमद फ़ैज़
दस्त-ए-तह-ए-संग

Contents

The Map 1
The Kaomao 3
Samyukta at Khajuraho 7
The Bed Book 8
Lie of the Land: A Letter to Chatwin 9
Enchilida 11
Stain 12
Making Out 13
Sarojini Naidu and She 14
'Our foster-nurse of nature is repose' 15
Alphabets of Nature 16
At Fourteen 17
The Salesman 18
Partying 19
Joyride 21
Discord 22
Man on the Make 23
Feb. 1944. Kasturba Talks of Life with Gandhi 24
Dust Storm in April 26
The Planetoid 27
The Word-worker 28
Daywatch in the Scriptorium 29
Parrots 30
Hotel Palm Grove, Bombay 31
The Drake 33
Monsoon Cantata 34

Arrival 35
The Fitness Fad 37
At Forty 38
Distance 39
Poetry 41
'According to my bond: no more nor less.' 43

The Map

It's a smallish piece of paper,
Twelve inches wide and nine in length.
It's hand drawn, with bright colours
Painted in. It's the map of an island.
The fine brown lines going round and round
Indicate the topography of mountains;
Varying shades of green denote the plains.
All around shimmers a stippled, blue-black sea,
And the curved coastline is dotted with
Green palms, some swaying in the breeze.
The map also reveals secrets, such as
The direction in which the wind will blow,
Where the dark clouds will gather,
Where it will pour.
The dead centre demarcates the territory
Of a volcano, unexpected and puzzling.
Geophysicists peer into its smoking vent,
Wondering how, for over a thousand years,
It's been fuming yet never allowed
Its seething discontents to spew out.
Sometimes lava boils and collects
At the lip of the gaping mouth.
It never brims over. It just flows back.
The volcanists fall over one another,
In order to be the first to discover
Where all the lava comes from
And where it goes back.

The Kaomao

That day, I fell off
The Pawmaw tree,
Plop, into the sea.
As the waves whisked me away
I strained to catch a last glimpse
Of the squat-boled tree
That had birthed and borne me.

Drifting away, I saw
Its branches coiled and hooded
Like cobras; the club-shaped
Leaves that topped them
Were emerald-green.
And, of the three fruit
That had dangled from the tree,
I was the one that was swung
Off-shore by a high wind
That tore me off the branch
That snaked over the sea.

That surf was gentle; the
Monsoon drift warm and easy.
I travelled slowly: sleeping,
At times, wide awake.
Fish came and lunged at me,
Felt my bristles and were gone.
Mostly, I chatted with the stars . . .

I don't know anything about
Minutes, hours and days,
Though, I'm knowledgeable

About seasons, where time
Travels leisurely. I've begun
To feel a little cold.
So, I gather, I'm in the grip
Of the South Indian Current
Carrying me on
Towards the Pacific.

Imagine, a vast watery bed
Lulling you; travelling —
Sleeping, waking; nothing
In sight other than an
Occasional migrant bird
(Poor fellow! he must be tired).
Sometimes, shoals of fish yapping,
Berating their leader for having
Led them into cold waters . . .

How should I know the seasons?
The sea's salt doesn't change.
Birds and fish don't mess around
With a peculiar-looking fruit . . .
I see no land, no sand, no trees . . .

Today, the waves are breakers;
They're hurling me forward
And pulling me back. It seems
They're cannonading into something,
Yes! I think it's land . . .

We've circumambulated this island.
It's this northern side that seems
To have the site for a fair anchorage.
Now, I'm quite close to the shore,
A poor strip of grey beach —

And I see this man; bearded,
Wizened, trousers rolled up —
He's fishing . . .

He's made a netted fishing basket
By weaving together spikes of
Palm leaves. He's set up the basket
At the end of a pole. He's repeatedly
Dipping it into the sea.
He's spotted me; his eager eyes glow.
This small eddy is pushing me
Into the basket. I'm going in, I'm gone . . .

I'm in the company of lobsters
Who've shied away from me.
I'm being carried ashore.
When did I last see
Rocks, sand, trees . . . ?
He's muttering to himself . . .
Something like, 'By God!
Selanderx Kirkale's* going to eat
Something different today . . . '
This man is going to eat me.

When will he eat me?
Bite into me; tear out
And spit away the bristles?
He'll sink his teeth into my
Outer juicy pulp . . .
Will he be utterly surprised
By my thin inner lining
Of matted hair?

That may ruin his sense of taste . . .
Fuel his serendipity,

Excite his anger . . .
Will he strip the core
Of the seed-hair to encounter
Again, juicy, fruity pulp?
Slurp, bite hard, and perhaps,
Have an incisor or two hurt,
By my heart-of-stone,
Pip-centre . . . ?

* Selanderx Kirkale — an anagram for Alexander Selkirk, (1676–1721). A Scottish sailor who was the prototype of Robinson Crusoe.

Samyukta at Khajuraho

(For Shubha Mudgal)

Nineteen is an impressionable age.
Monuments, March nights, spin a
world of their own. You emerge from
the sanctum on to the pillared porch
of the temple. *Varnam, pallavi, moksha,*
we watch transfixed, impaled by the
stirrings of adolescent delight.
Next morning, we're there at your

hotel, autograph books in hand.
You answer our timid knock: petite,
hair dishevelled, your English shaky.
The magic wears off. And we, afflicted
by the wand's light touch, terminally
ill with aesthesia, wander off to
recapture tenuous beauty in word
and in song.

The Bed Book

In mother's bedtime tales,
The scenario is always the same,
When lightning strikes.
Night, thunder, rain; seen
During intermittent flashes,
Wisp of road through tall grass.
When the blaze finally decides
To descend either on hump of hill,
Lost child, or tree quietly
Growing, the object is always
Alone. Mother never lets me know
Whether it screams as it goes,
A supersonic bleep humans never hear,
And children sense in a series of poised pictures.

Now, grown-up,
Lightning strikes are a part
Of inviolable routine. No wild,
Uncharted terrain but the town's
Main street. Bicycles, rickshaws,
Low-slung automobiles, the sun
In its place. In a high-browed
Hall snazzy with alcove, fireplace,
Pen and ink sketches of Chesterton,
Lamb, Blake *et al.*, lightning sans
Flash, fire or din. Or smell of charring . . .

Mother, thank you,
For the fairy tale.

The Lie of the Land: A Letter to Chatwin

If I were to set stock
In your words Bruce,
If, as you deduce,
Man is migratory,
Maybe I'd venture to say
That land is meant
For aerial viewing.

Upright, I'm uptight; I hardly
Ever range beyond my nose. Avian,
On my belly, I'd at least see
The ditches, gullies, promontories,
Foot-wide streams cutting deep
Into cartilage and bone of soil,
Camouflaged by thickets.
Land never fails to surprise.
What I perceive as a stable
Patch of green may very well
Decline to bear dead weight,
And instead, have my legs flail
In a void. Or, as I brace myself
For a mile of arduous ascent, the
Mountain may decide to become the
Shoulder of a hill; there, where I'd
Envisaged an apex, may lie a
Plateau-like ridge; a pine-encrusted
Slope may give me the slip
And have me come down hard —
Down to the very rock-bottom.

All muscle and bone, my legs feel
Responsible for most of my bad-hair
Days. If I were a creepy-crawly,
Or an airy-fairy, I'd at least
Stick to instincts; never dare;
Nor feel piqued at the bamboo's
Jointed stilts able to
Wave to the sun, bow to the wind.

Enchilida

She wonders if she'll ever know
This man.
Five or fifteen years of marriage,
He's still a closed fist.

She's read up the pages of
His desires, aches, insomnia;
His fear of loneliness
Grips him like the stare
Of a single red bird-eye.

She's devoured him up . . .
Sent him reeling through
The undergrowth blinded and
Disarmed by pain . . .
Then she's followed him . . .

Through separations and miraculous
Recoveries, misery and camaraderie,
The yarn they've spun has slubbed.
Maybe the two are strangers, still,
She incessantly ponders,
What is it he wants?
What may she give him?

Stain

A monsoon month. A grey unbroken sky,
heavy with clouds. Under a croton I'm
grafting. I whittle away half an inch
of hide, expose the xylem dull-white
as bone. Apply hormone powder, dress
the wound with moss, wrap a piece of
plastic, secure it with twine. I'll
wait a fortnight for the sap to
weave roots for the clone.

I come in for a bath. Undress, gape at
my blouse. A russet stain on the left
shoulder. Plant juice surreptitiously
seeped into the fabric, spread, took on
its texture. Scrubbing with soap and
water, using a mild stain remover,
heightens the colour; firming up a faith
in the power of bonding.

Making Out

As always, below a benign
sun, under a wide-open sky,
trees dozing in the wind,

we make love;
no bodies touching, not a sound:
locked-in eyes . . .

You shrink into yourself. All of
your six feet seem to be folding
up. Your loose clothes are flapping
in the wind —

Your scooter helmet's foam inner
lining is torn. You are greying.
You are balding. You're tongue-tied
and blushing —

A teenager overwhelmed by
his first love.

Sarojini Naidu and She

She casts about; tries to get a grip —
Shocked at the sodden similarities
Of lives with separate histories,
Somehow on the same bloody trip.
Why should the two of them flip
Their lids for men much older; ignoring
ground reality,
Wishing to compose poetry, as if the hilarity
Of the first choice isn't enough to have
them labelled hip?

Indian women poets are plump; never thought
of as bright.
They're packed off to Oxbridge when the one
They want to marry is deemed the wrong guy.

At Oxbridge, some Englishman teaches them
right.
With their clutch of poems, they head back
for the Indian sun,
Marry their old fogey; make the family
tut-tut and sigh . . .

'Our foster-nurse of nature is repose'

Lying in bed on a pure-white sheet, the
air-conditioner whirring, I stare at the
strip light and when my eyes smart
I turn and it seems, for the first time,
I consider your features.

Eyelashes like an aunt's, inked and curled;
mouth petulant, the shape of your limbs
like your father's. Not even your
temper matches mine.

Wheat-gold child, sleeping.
You assure me that I belong to
the land of *karma*. Having performed my
duty why should I wish that my shadow,
like a stamp, should brand you?

What gesture of atonement can I make?
You whom I've flogged in dreams each
time you upset an apple-cart with a
sneeze or fever?

Let me clear this room of frost and fire,
shoo away clamour, turn out the light that
drills through your lids. What can I give you,
before the world claims you, but
these few hours of uninterrupted sleep?

Alphabets of Nature

He looks at a serrated oak leaf;
Smells it, rubs its smooth white
Underside against my cheek,
Then flings it away. He moves on,
Discovers flowers on the hill,
Their genera for him as yet unnamed.
He pulls out the pistils, dips
The stigmas into the pollen,
Takes the anthers apart.
I can see him, years later,
Examining a body . . .
Son, will you, by chance,
Recollect, the insular glory
Of your father inviolate
In his separate bedroom,
The day you tire of your wife?

At Fourteen

Draped on the day-bed,
Watching her walk across
To settle a wall-picture gone askew,
One day when he was fourteen,
He said, *Mum! you're ungainly* . . .
He was grinning . . .

In the clear air
Of the quiet living-room,
On the handcrafted teapoy,
A plaster-cast of 'Yakshi with Lotus'
Continued with its shut-eyed
Half smile . . .
Her ormulu Ditmar oil-lamp glowed . . .

She was sitting by his head, reading . . .
He half rose, twined a lock
Of her greying hair round
His index finger . . .
Your hair has grown . . .
It looks nice . . . he said.

The Salesman

Making sure there's no one around
I confront the first, lift my right
Leg high, miss the mark, hear in the
Silent stairwell the flat sound of
A shoed foot striking stone; in my
Mouth the well known, indefinable
Taste of a tap run dry.
Right angled, poker face perfect

Stairs, sentinelled by a set of
Walls speeding along, taken by
Surprise at each fall and rise,
Thrown completely out of gear
At every fleshed out corner.
What am I doing here? My finger
On a bell, *Bing-bong*. The cut-out
Of a door introducing a

Space, framing a face; the initial,
Quizzical look hardening into a
Stare; a disembodied
Syllable *Yes ?* drilling a hole
At a certain place: I visualize
The contortions of a half-loose
Paper poster on a wall,
Madly flapping in the wind.

Partying

Entering the room, glad at
Not having stumbled in,
Thankfully I'm blinded
By candlelight, muffled
By haze; am comforted
By my almost immediate
Re-entry into my

Own private daze. From such
A point of vantage shall
I savour the scene; see,
Select, discard at ease
These objects set up for
Me. Weighted by drapery
The windows have shut down

Their lids. A glass-panelled
Door opens out on to
A balcony. Against
The backdrop of night the
Marble balusters gleam
Like teeth with gaps in
Between. Further off, a

Scrim of libertine cloud
Floats in and begins to
Dissipate itself for
A self-absorbed moon.
Men's talk of stocks and shares.
The latest in fast cars:
The women discussing

Perfumery in carefully
Cultivated, cultured
Semitones. Crystal and
Jewel wink in the wan
Light. Null, washed out of words,
I catch the chirrup of
A cricket well-hidden

In the terrace shrubbery.
Don't hesitate: Participate,
Someone will urge. Someone
Will turn on the music.
Shall I glide or swim, twirl,
Trill as the world closes
In? Left foot forward, bent

At the knee, left hand thrust
Out for balance, shall I
Surf up a crest, slide down
To a trough, drown or swell,
Buy or sell or should I
Reverberate in my empty shell?

Joyride

(for Papa)

You take us for a crazy jeep ride,
Show us sights you now cannot yourself see,
Till daylight fades out on every side.

Fighting diabetes, your time you bide:
Meanwhile, our zestful guide you wish to be,
You take us for a crazy jeep ride.

Past Kempty Falls, Yamuna Bridge, we ride.
The dirt track's disappearing, it seems to me,
As daylight fades out on every side.

Autumn's palette is generous. Far and wide,
Rice-sown terrace-fields are a lush olive-green.
You take us for a crazy jeep ride.

On roofs, chillies undergo a drying rite,
Festoons of corn on the cob wag in the breeze,
Till daylight fades out on every side.

At Thathyoud, you surprise us; you recite —
It is a beauteous evening, calm and free. . . .
You take us for a crazy jeep ride,
Till daylight fades out on every side.

Discord

She sits on a rattan chair,
I, opposite her, on the sofa.
Between us, on the covered floor,
our two boys play war games.
Floral arrangements on the
ersatz Persian rug unroll
before my eyes; her rigid spine,
the way she concentrates
on her needlepoint.
Her secret pain comes gushing out.
Unable to do or say anything
I explore inter-stellar space
in a bid to fix the design.
They've been at it again
Like two crossed knives, husband and wife.

Man on the Make

I shall paint a man on the make.
In his late forties, five feet five,
One stone eye, portly.
Standing in a hall of mirrors he sees

Everywhere only himself, choosing
Not to see the profile: sagging cheek
And chin, the nose too long. He hears
Himself speak, only

His voice as people come and go.
In the hall, on the mirrored north wall,
A clear window. Beyond the window,
A rush of open plain, finally resting

At the foot of a mountain range.
Above the furrowed mountains, a sky
Changing colours. Window, plain, mountain,
Sky, agape at the man on the make.

Feb. 1944. Kasturba Talks of Life with Gandhi

. . . He began to mumble . . .
This thing that rages within me,
I must kill it . . .
It's not that I don't desire you,
I still do, but, it affects
my concentration, my assiduousness;
Ba, you must understand . . .

I was only half-listening.
My back to him, squatting
On the floor, I was bending
Over the coal-stove,
Worrying about my Ramdas' fever . . .

He'd always been a bit odd.
Seven times round a fire
And we were wed . . .
Now, I'll live the life
of a celibate. I'll feed and
clothe you, and that's that . . .

Back in India for good —
Once again, there was travelling,
Meetings, satyagrahas, and when
That thing raged within me
I would stand behind a curtain
And gaze at young Jawahar,
Or, the stodgy Patel . . .

Sometimes, one of them would
Look up. Then, I'd have to
Leave; from behind some barred window
Watch the light angle across
The yard. It's not our practice to
Shut doors for privacy. And, I was
Too correct to recall that one
Childhood memory, when, bathing
In the creek, half a mile off
The town, my friend Mithu and I,
Both of us then aged nine,
Had deliberately,
Out of sheer curiosity,
Touched each other in places —
All the while giggling uncontrollably . . .

Dust Storm in April

6:30 in the evening,
Down Hastings Road,
There's dull light hovering
Over the Polo Ground.

It brews. Puffs of silk-cotton,
Flame-coloured petals,
Eucalyptus bark, eddies of dust,
Then, it's lights-out.

Through the haze, blinding
Headlights catch the walkers
Hurrying; plump, middle-aged
Women in trainers, trying to
Outrun the storm.

A gang of boys on bicycles
Lets out howls of delight;
Acts, as if in a rodeo,
They're on bucking broncos.

The cattle heading home
Seem unworried. Two young bulls
Spar. Their cows continue
To chew on paper and polythene
Foraged from a public bin.

The Planetoid

It drifts slowly, dreaming. This is
No straight and narrow path but an
Orbit with no signposts at the
Bends. The planetoid senses it —
A shower of meteorites awaits it.
At first a rock fragment or two.
Later, full-scale bombardment that
Might take in its wake a portion
Of its crust. The planetoid is
Accustomed to these astroblemes.
What it fears is plate tectonics.
Words shifting then falling into
Place but not without having first
Created gaps, fissures, chasms,
Other kinds of yawning space. The
Planetoid wishes to avoid
Disfigurement. But it cannot
Veer out of a predestined course.

The Word-worker

My eyes lick them off the page;
I chew them, suck the juices,
Let the flavours seep in. I am
The dreamer; words, the cocoon
I knit. Fixed for ever in the
Slim gap between alphabets
I am the saboteur, the hit-man.
Words scurry down dark lanes
Or brightly lit streets. I rip
Off masks, bequeath new skin,
Dragoon words into birthing
Faces never before born.

Daywatch in the Scriptorium

The guests have departed.
The raging fever gone.
This blank page beckons me
To give it something of myself.

Oak leaves turn in the wind,
Moss-green on silver. The
Mesh of needles on a coniferous
Branch, flat as a palm, strains
The sunlight. Behind a hill, it
Seems as if an invisible Indian
Chief has hunkered down to puff
Out spreading clouds of peace.
A rufous-throated nuthatch
Is disappointed. The apples
Are small, hard and green.
It flies away boring through
Haze and rows of hills.

Fair, weather, like a leafed twig
Suddenly landing at my feet,
Don't welsh on me. Alchemic
Day in June, live on in memory.

Parrots

What do you know
Of the fragrant oils
That seep out of her cells
At the sight of a pair
Of parrots in flight.

Jets of green, they arc,
Swerve, rise up and dive,
Dip and rise, alight
On a mango branch,
Sit side by side, and,
Thus arranged, proceed to
Peck at each others' necks —
Using their beaks like the
Teeth of a blood-red comb,
Groom each other, head to toe . . .

There . . . he's licking her throat,
Burying his head between her breasts,
He's suckling them like
Sucking on ripe mangoes . . .
Here, he's at her navel . . .
He's sloshing his tongue around . . .
He's turned her over . . .
Nips at the back of her shoulders,
Bites all down her spine,
Now, he's using his hands to knead her . . .

The parrots are beak to beak.
Her fragrant oils alight, she seeks
The metallic aroma of blue-black ink
Streaming on paper . . .
Her saliva has a sour, astringent taste . . .

Hotel Palm Grove, Bombay

I'm fighting for space.
In a double-occupancy room
I'm squabbling for space.

A copper-coloured Shivaji,
His two young sons and a cannon,
Look out at the Arabian sea;
As also, the bored maitre d',
A sweepress in a
Red on white print sari,
The blonde 8 a.m. jogger in blue shorts
Who's got out of her just-parked car.

Crows — some ten or fifteen of them,
Fly out of the grey-blue towards me.
One of them perches on the tuft
Of Shivaji's turban.
While the cleft saffron flag
Behind the statuary
Continues to brandish,
In room 114
I fight for space
Doggedly . . .

I'm fighting for a space
Where an image of your face
Won't intrude . . .
The plateau of your broad forehead,
Two blue veins swelling up,
One travelling north,
The other north-east,
Two ridges riding off
Into the forest of your
Wiry grey-white hair;
Your eyebrows, untidy,
Tweaked at the ends;
Your too-long nose, an outcrop;
Your thin upper lip, I suck out
From behind your moustache
When I kiss you . . .

Even as we fall
Upon the bed
I'm fighting
For space . . .

A space for words . . .

Wish-granting words,
My gigolos . . .

The Drake

On one of my many sojourns I shall
Chance upon the silk of water, rippling.
The tall, unstaid grasses will sway. My wings
Shall nudge and part the air. I shall circle
And dive, confident of a smooth landing.
North America and Siberia are prey
To an insidious cold that works its
Way into the limbs and dampens my wings.
Tropical heat blanches and sears; my golds
Greens and browns weaken. Besides, I detest
Crowded lakes, the enervating pressures
Of communitarian living, the
Constant cackle of dissatisfactions.
I recall the taste of many waters
Yet a thirst persists. My trajectory
Is wide but circular. The sooner I
Accept this the better. Why is it I
Tire, feel old and abject? Should I
Give up migrations, settle down to rest?

Monsoon Cantata

Rain is tattooing on the roof, tap-tapping
On the tin sunshade of the kitchen window,
Beating an insistent though erratic rhythm,
Deranged by dancing leaves that come in its
Way, like a chorus of mad women that seems to
Say — drench us, O drench us.

Across the barred, shut gate the road is
Gold and silver under the benign glare
Of sodium and fluorescent lamps; crimson
Tail-lights, tyres swish past. Criss-cross
Wires chip. A quiver of quicksilver water
Is rushing towards the gate — the barred, shut gate.

Something is knocking down that gate,
Something in connivance with the rain,
I turn my back to it, stare steadfastly
At the gas burner, at the metal frame of
its round head with pricked-in holes.
Something has knocked down the gate,
Contralto voices come storming in,
Suicide-squad assassinations, communal
Conflagrations, scams, arms deals, a tribal
Woman gang-raped, mute deaths in custody,
India in the nineteen nineties. Something
Has knocked down a gate.

I turn on the gas,
Flare like the many
Blue, incandescent flames.

Arrival

Within this hotel room,
at this point in time,
I stand beside him.

Under the tall lancet window,
through stained glass,
I see heat waves rise;
He — forests of black pine.

Some hundred feet below us,
on the busy motorway,
red double-decker coaches
appear to him — blue.

Now will we turn to face this room?

In the far left corner
a plush burgundy bed
(we'll sink into);
leopard-skin sofa;
a fawn-coloured carpet
(tickles the soles of my naked feet);
straight-backed chairs, two;
a four-cornered winking eye,
softly blathering news . . .

When will I mention the lace-covered,
lion's paw table, tucked away on my right?

On it, long-stemmed glasses,
bottles of wine, cheeses,

a statuette of Rodin's *The kiss,*
a bowl of fruit . . .

And the missing champagne bottle,
will it on its own uncork, froth, spew,
when, into some other room, I walk in
at another point in time,
clutching to my bosom
a swaddled little-boy-blue?

The Fitness Fad

Growing fat, I worry,
Quite naturally, take to
Running east to west,
North to south. Worry
Some more as the adipose
Dissolves; can't help feel
I wouldn't mind very
Much, if, in the
Ultimate analyses,
There's much more of me
Than svelte contemporaries.
So, end it all, in the process
Having made, quite by chance,
Fence-sitting a fine art.

At Forty

At forty she finds out how redundant emotion
is in the living of life. At nine —
the passing away of a puppy: sobbing the only option.
At sixteen, heartbreak: her boyfriend whines
he's leaving town. At twenty-one she tells herself
now she's too
grown-up; learns to transpose distress to a
pinching shoe.

At thirty-three her marriage is nosediving;
the extended family is weighing
down heavily upon her. Her children are
fractious. Colleagues are vicious. Her car
breaks down very often. The WC is
clogged. At thirty-eight she loses her dad
to diabetes.

Crying gets her nowhere. Tears have lost their zing.
Malleable-mop-up-mom has become a rational thing.

Distance

(For Primo Levi)

Across the seven seas (as gran'ma would've said),
it hits me, 'Coup in Pakistan: Indian Army
On Red Alert', informs *The Independent* . . .

At the pay-phone, waiting for the student to finish
His call, I concentrate on the vending machine
Asking me to make my choice, put in the coins,
Punch in my selection only after the red
Light stops blinking . . . outside it's nippy . . .

The maples and chestnuts have begun to turn colour.
Mists have now come down to stay. On the lawn, ducks,
  drakes,
A single swan, squabble over an abandoned
Baguette, while the unblinking Loch Airthrey
Tries to suck in some weak October sun . . .

The Loch's shirred surface, the boy's difficult-to-decipher
Falkirk burr, the hum and whirr of the vending machine,
BT eating up my hard-earned pounds sterling, I shout
Into the receiver asking, *Sab kuch theek hai . . . ?*

'Militaristic nation with a point to prove',
Says Ranjan Gupta in *The Herald* 'World News'.

Surely General Musharraf won't unleash a nuclear
Warhead on Allahabad? Blow into dust
High-roofed 8A Hastings Road, the match-box
Jyoti Apartments, or, colourful, crowded, noisy,

Chowk with its wynds? Nor rip off earth's tapestry
The mud-brown and moss-green skeins of the Ganges
And the Yamuna — unknot the Sangam? Unloose the
Subterranean Saraswati and vapourize it?
Convert to desert one of civilization's
Oldest cities venerated by Harsha Siladitya,
Chronicled by Hsuang-tsang, toured by back-packing
  Europeans,
Americans, Australians, in their bid to assimilate the East?

And I, survive the holocaust, as I'm away
In Scotland, working out the plot of a story
Wherein the twain shall meet . . . ?

Poetry

This Sunday, once again, I come back to you, love,
All my cares cast aside — the child struggling with his O levels;
My dreamy, difficult husband; the old man who said,
Come child, come, then pushed me down the hill . . .

In the light rain, I walk down Giles Lane to St Stephen's Hill,
And take the footpath to Little Hall Farm, Eastingdown, Alcroft Grange . . .
Squelch over fallen chestnut and oak leaves till I come to Little Hall Pinetum
And see conifers, green sails in a sea of brown dead ferns . . .
Am surprised by a white Citreon Romahome with trailer, sitting
Patiently outside a brick house with a Tudor beam facade
The house quietly smoking in the rain, in winter . . .

Sheep-come-near-the-fence move off, turn around and stare at me.
I walk on to where the single track potholed road turns into a path,
Wind my way on till a neighing unsettles me . . . I see it . . .
Big, black, powerful, nostrils smoking . . . It snorts. I make a move
Towards it. It shakes its mane, neighs again and walks till it's behind
A bush from where it watches . . . What does it see, dear horse?
An oddball in an anorak with an eskimo hood?
I'm just as nervy . . . What if it breaks out and tramples me?

It's to you I return, tired and hungry . . . It's with you I
wrestle . . .
Like a man I shout at you . . . , when you lay down the
wrong preposition,
Dish out a difficult verb, throw a tantrum over a metaphor
I'd spent so much
Energy inventing . . . Yes, we quarrel. You fling your history
and pedigree
In my face and I say, *Get out I don't want you . . .*

It'll go on for hours, won't it love?
Till we're exhausted and my fingers ache?

Hopefully, by then, the weather will have cleared . . .

'According to my bond: no more nor less.'

The universe is intentionless.
The wind blows, stars collapse.
Day becomes night and night
Becomes day. Flowers in the garden
Bloom and fruit rots despite me.
I worry of why the scarlet rose
Fades, why the calendula does not
Grow a bigger head. I am no more
Than a head full of random thoughts.
The brain is intentionless. The synapse
Receives and transmits a command.
A limb moves regardless of whether
It is raised for good or bad.